128 Billion to 1

128
Billion
TO 1

How to Dramatically Improve Your Odds
of Winning an Unfair Bet

MIKE NEMETH

NEW YORK

LONDON • NASHVILLE • MELBOURNE • VANCOUVER

128 Billion to 1

Ten Steps to Beat the Odds and Win Your NCAA Tourney Office Pool

© 2018 Mike Nemeth

Published in New York, New York, by Morgan James Publishing. Morgan James is a trademark of Morgan James, LLC. www.MorganJamesPublishing.com

The Morgan James Speakers Group can bring authors to your live event. For more information or to book an event visit The Morgan James Speakers Group at www.TheMorganJamesSpeakersGroup.com.

ISBN 9781683506355 paperback
ISBN 9781683506362 eBook
Library of Congress Control Number: 2017909729

Cover and Interior Design by:
Chris Treccani
www.3dogcreative.net

In an effort to support local communities, raise awareness and funds, Morgan James Publishing donates a percentage of all book sales for the life of each book to Habitat for Humanity Peninsula and Greater Williamsburg.

Get involved today! Visit www.MorganJamesBuilds.com

For Pops

He taught me that life is a competitive sport.

Table of Contents

Introduction
128 Billion to 1

Each year 70 million people—some fans, some seasonal thrill-seekers—fill out brackets predicting the winners of the sixty-three college basketball games that comprise the NCAA Men's College Basketball Tournament—March Madness™. And, every year the brackets are covered in red ink denoting all the wrong guesses. The odds against filling a perfect bracket are 128 billion to 1. Hence the name of this modest tome.

128 billion is a big number. If every man, woman and child alive today on earth were to fill 18 brackets, and if every bracket were unique, one would be perfect. A computer could do it (by filling 128 billion unique brackets), but

no human would submit the one that would ultimately be correct. It would not be believable.

This book will outline all the reasons why no human has ever, why no human will likely ever, fill a perfect bracket. It has less to do with making intelligent choices and more to do with the unfortunate digestion of the misinformation surrounding the tournament. This book will argue that no expert today has the tools, the knowledge, or the clairvoyance to advise fans on picks. This book will also suggest the best ways to mitigate the effects of misinformation and will suggest a tool that would improve the odds of filling a winning—not perfect—bracket.

Chapter One

The Black Swan

All truth passes through three stages.
First, it is ridiculed.
Second, it is violently opposed.
Third, it is accepted as being self-evident.
—ARTHUR SCHOPENHAUER

On a frigid February evening in 2003, David slew Goliath once again. Or so it must have seemed to countless couch potatoes across the nation who spent that evening watching the televised college basketball game between the Wisconsin Badgers and the Michigan State Spartans. The Badgers and Spartans had become fierce rivals in the struggle to dominate the Big Ten Conference, and the results of this game would eventually determine that season's

1

conference champion. On this night, the game was played in Madison, Wisconsin, where barhopping students scurried down State Street with the razor-sharp prairie air rattling in their lungs like ice cubes in a martini shaker. Inside the gaudy new Kohl Center, seventeen thousand overheated fans screamed in anticipation of the battle between the highly regarded Spartans and the upset-minded Badgers.

The Spartans have a storied basketball history that includes two national championships that still resonate in our collective memory. Their 1979 championship season culminated with the legendary battle between Magic Johnson and Larry Bird, the battle that presaged the rebirth of the National Basketball Association. Their 2000 season also had a storybook ending for future Hall of Fame Coach Tom Izzo and several key players from the depressed community of Flint, Michigan. Before the 2003 season began, basketball trade magazines predicted that the Spartans would win the Big Ten Conference championship, and two national polls ranked the Spartans in the pre-season Top 25. Michigan

State was loaded with talent and coached by a man at the top of his profession.

By contrast, most fans would be shocked to learn that the 1941 NCAA Championship banner flies from the Kohl Center rafters. More recently, the Badgers reached the NCAA Tournament's Final Four in 2000 and won the Big Ten title in 2002. Nonetheless, the Wisconsin basketball team labored in relative anonymity. The basketball trade magazines picked the Badgers to finish fourth in the Big Ten Conference race and predicted they would fail to make the national championship tournament field. Michigan State was perceived to be an excellent basketball program; Wisconsin was perceived to be mediocre. And that's why the Spartans played Goliath and the Badgers played David in this drama on the plains in February of 2003.

As I watched the action from the comfort of a recliner a thousand miles to the Southeast, an array of conflicting sensations and impressions assaulted me. The Spartans moved swiftly and fluidly up and down the court, punctuating their stylistic play with crowd-pleasing dunks, while the Badgers moved slowly and cautiously, taking few risks and making few dramatic plays. Michigan State played with confidence and a graceful economy of effort. Repeatedly they brought the ball down the floor, tossed it inside to a big man, and scored easily. Wisconsin, on the other hand, dribbled aimlessly, passed the ball around the perimeter, settled for outside shots, and missed more often than not. When the Badgers did penetrate the Spartan defense, Michigan State punished them with hard fouls.

But this isn't so much a story about David and Goliath as it is a story about a slingshot and a stone. According to the play-by-play announcers, Michigan State held the advantage in all the important statistical categories, including shooting percentage and rebounds, yet the halftime scoreboard showed that the neighborhood kids were leading by four points!

As the second half unfolded, I sensed that something inexplicable but fascinating was happening on the floor of the cavernous Kohl Center. Although the Spartans continued to score effortlessly when they could get the ball into the front court, they squandered chance after chance to pull even with the Badgers. As the minutes ticked away, Spartan composure bled away like water evaporating in the Mojave Desert.

The Badgers seemed to labor for points, yet each time the Spartans threatened to close the gap, a Wisconsin player made a timely three-pointer, or a "garbage" basket off a missed shot, or two free throws after a gratuitous foul. Although the announcers constantly reminded the viewing audience that the Spartans were shooting the lights out and controlling the backboards, the Badgers methodically pulled away on the scoreboard. Eventually the clock became the Spartans' enemy, and they were forced to foul the Badgers on every trip down the floor. Free throws, however, are the province of players of little renown. The Badgers strode confidently to the line and drove the final nails into the Spartans' coffin. Final score: Badgers 64, Spartans 53.

Although the Badgers were tied for first place in the Big Ten, the experts didn't consider the team worthy of a ranking in the weekly Top 25. That respect wouldn't be paid to the team until three weeks later when they secured a second consecutive Big Ten title. Contrary to expert predictions, Wisconsin did receive an invitation to the NCAA Tournament and reached the prestigious Sweet Sixteen. They didn't play the game as supposedly good teams played it, didn't have a roster studded with high school All-Americans, didn't look fearsome walking through airports, and didn't have a famous coach—yet they produced better results than most other teams.

"It's elementary, my dear Watson"

On television that night, the sports juggernaut raced onward: games, scores, highlights, analysis—a veritable intravenous drip for the addicted. The recap of the Badgers' game was brisk and trite and did little to explain how an underdog had managed to win a game in which it apparently had shot poorly and been outrebounded in the bargain. To satisfy my curiosity, I checked the box score and verified the basic stats: Michigan State had shot 52.4 percent from the floor, better than the collegiate average and impressive on the road; Wisconsin had shot a paltry 37 percent, dismal for a home team and unusual for a winning team. Michigan State had also outrebounded the Badgers 30-27, a deficit that had been narrowed in the waning minutes as the Spartans missed desperation shots. These basic statistics are the essence of the game, and we've all been conditioned to believe that a team will win when producing these statistical advantages. Yet, these advantages had produced a stone in the forehead for Michigan State.

A closer look at the statistics revealed two shocking numbers: 1) the Badgers had taken twelve more shots from the floor than did the Spartans (54 to 42), and 2) the Badgers had been given twelve more free throw attempts than the Spartans (22 to 10). My first thought: A team didn't need to be very good to win a game in which it had been given twenty-four more chances to score than its opponent. My more considered reaction: Perhaps a team had to be very good to manufacture twenty-four more chances to score.

The advantage implied by comparing 52.4 percent shooting to 37 percent shooting is valid only if the two percentages are applied to the same number of shot attempts. This is an elementary mathematical principle most of us are taught in grammar school, but announcers tend to use the shorthand notation of shooting percentage to describe the action in a game whether it is apropos or not.

Since Wisconsin took twelve more shots than Michigan State, the disparity in shooting percentage only produced two more baskets for the Spartans than the Badgers had made. As if that weren't enough to render the raw shooting percentage untrustworthy, the statistic combines two-point shots attempted and made with three-point shots attempted and made in a single percentage, as though all baskets counted the same number of points. The Badgers hit the mark on seven three-point baskets, while the Spartans could convert only three of the more valuable field goals. Thus, the two additional two-point baskets the Spartans had scored were exactly offset by the four additional points the Badgers had scored on three-point baskets. Despite the apparent disparity in the quality of shooting, the two teams had scored precisely the same number of points from the floor: forty-seven!

The impressive Spartan dunks made the highlight reel, while the Badgers' three-pointers weren't exciting enough to replay—but the splashy Spartan slams were barely enough to keep pace with the Badgers' long-range bombs. Comparing dunks to three-pointers in basketball is like comparing field artillery shells to tactical nuclear weapons—although they are both shot from the same cannon (hand), the difference in impact is devastating. In this respect, fans are conditioned to accept entertainment as a substitute for facts.

The only conclusion that can be drawn from this simple analysis of the field goals attempted and scored is that shooting percentage wasn't a critical factor in the outcome of this game, but the number of shots attempted certainly was. In the world of hockey, "shots on goal" is an important measure of team play and a statistic routinely kept to explain why one team won a game and the other lost. The idea is that a certain percentage of shots is going to get past even the best goalie, so a measure of the quality of the defense is the number of shot attempts it allows and, therefore, asks its goalie to deflect. Basketball statistics are less sophisticated and basketball announcers and analysts are either less sophisticated than hockey announcers and analysts or, perhaps, feel that basketball fans aren't sophisticated enough to appreciate the subtleties hidden by the shooting percentage statistic. So, a single number—52.4 percent—characterized the Spartans' shooting performance as "good," and a single number—37 percent—characterized the Badgers' shooting performance as "poor," when, in fact, the performances were identical: forty-seven points scored from the floor.

The question that logically follows from the shooting percentage analysis: How did the Badgers get twelve more shots on goal than the Spartans? In a basketball game possessions are traded evenly from tip-off to final horn so there can't be more than a single possession difference between the competitors. However, three circumstances produce differences in shots on goal within an equal number of ball possessions: turnovers (empty possessions that change from one team to the other before the team with the ball can take a shot on goal); possessions that result in free throws rather than an official shot on goal; and offensive rebounds of missed shots that allow the offensive team to have second and third chances to take a shot on goal.

During this game, the Spartans surrendered the ball before taking a shot on fifteen occasions—not an outrageous number of turnovers—but the Badgers committed only five turnovers of their own—a spectacularly low number of mistakes. In basketball, as in all team sports, everything is relative. Relatively speaking, a ten-turnover advantage transformed a level playing field (court) into a game tilted unfairly in Wisconsin's favor and supplied the Badgers with several additional shots on goal.

The Badgers earned seven second-chance shots on goal by snaring offensive rebounds and again enjoyed an advantage over the Spartans, who managed just four offensive rebounds. Thus, by taking care of the basketball and grabbing offensive rebounds, the Badgers had had at least thirteen more ball possessions than did the Spartans.

The *coup de grâce* was delivered at the charity stripe. The physical defensive play of the tough guys from East Lansing, a style of play much admired by the game's announcers, precipitated twenty-five whistles for infractions of the no-grabbing, no-pushing, no-climbing-over-the-back rules, and the Badgers were awarded twenty-two free throws in retribution. These shots are called free throws because a player gets ten seconds to aim a shot from just fifteen feet away without any defensive interference. The Badgers did well with these easy shots and padded their scoreboard total by seventeen points. Michigan State received only ten free throws as compensation for Wisconsin's fourteen fouls, and the Spartans made just six of them. That eleven-point difference was the margin of victory.

Basically, this game was like a match between two gunfighters at high noon when only one opponent has bullets in his pistol—the Spartans literally had no chance to win the fight.

So what of the rebounding advantage the Spartans produced? Year after year, they are listed among the very best rebounding teams in the country, and their legendary toughness is typically credited with this prowess. In this game, they garnered twenty-six of their rebounds on the defensive end of the court, where the defensive team always has the advantage of blocking out the offensive players. Remember that the Badgers launched far more shots at the Spartans' goal than the other way around and missed more shots as well.

It becomes clear that the Spartans grabbed a lot of rebounds because they were presented with a lot more rebounding opportunities under their own basket. In other words, the team padded its rebounding total by giving up too many shots on goal, something for which hockey defenses would be roundly criticized. In fact, there were thirty-three misses on the Spartans' end of the floor, and the Badgers turned seven of them into second chances. Ergo, the Spartans' snatched 78.8 percent of the *available* rebounds. On the other end of the court, where the Badger defense limited the Spartans to far fewer shots, the Badgers grabbed twenty rebounds out of the twenty-four that were *available,* for a defensive rebounding percentage of 83.3 percent. Amazing as it may seem, despite the fact that the Spartans had more total rebounds, the Badgers did the better job of rebounding by posting a better defensive rebounding percentage and pulling down more offensive rebounds to boot.

Basketball is like a ballet—when the intricately interwoven athletic movements are combined at a fast pace with sharp, accurate ball movements, it is a thing of natural beauty that is pleasing to the eyes of fans, experts, and coaches. But the Badgers' slow pace of play, carefully controlled style, low shooting percentage, and general lack of athletic movements combine to make them appear less skilled, and certainly less entertaining, than other teams. The perception is that the Badgers play ugly and, therefore, play poorly.

According to the announcers, an underdog David and his slingshot had bested a fearsome Goliath once again. According to the traditional box score, Goliath fought well and didn't deserve its fate. More than a few fans attributed the Badger victory to the difficulty of winning on the road in the Big Ten, although the fans could not explain what was difficult about outshooting and outrebounding the home team. Still other fans referred to the Kohl Center as the Bermuda Triangle of college basketball, a place with the mystical power to confuse and disorient visiting teams. If we accept the premise that the winner of any game has played better than the loser, then we must accept the conclusion that the Badgers simply outplayed the Spartans. The experts' challenge is to identify the explanatory and deterministic factors that impact outcomes, but the experts steadfastly dismiss teams, playing styles, and game outcomes that do not fit their conventional, inside-the-box thinking. An old adage says you can't prove every swan is white, but with a single black swan you prove they are not. The Wisconsin/Michigan State game was a black swan.

The problem with traditional box scores is that the recorded statistics are merely the accumulation of raw individual effort, but they don't relate to, or correlate with, game results. For more than one hundred years after Dr. James Naismith nailed the peach basket to the barn wall, no one involved in the game had bothered to identify and measure the factors that determine and explain the outcome of games. So I decided to do it.

Chapter Two

Everything Is Relative

*What these geek numbers show—no prove—is
that the traditional yardsticks of success for
players and teams are fatally flawed.*
**—FROM THE JACKET COVER OF
MONEYBALL BY MICHAEL LEWIS**

Coincidentally, in 2003 Michael Lewis (The Blind Side, The Big Short) published his ground-breaking book about baseball, Moneyball, just as I began investigating how basketball really works. The basic premise of his book: Baseball "experts," coaches, managers, front office executives, players, and the media had collected and analyzed an exhaustive array of statistics about the game for more than one hundred years, and yet they had overlooked the statistics that were the keys to success at the game.

By employing advanced analytics, the Oakland A's Major League Baseball franchise deduced that a relatively new statistic called *on base percentage* (introduced in 1984) was a superior indicator of player value to the time-honored statistic called *batting average*. While batting average only credits a player with hits, on base percentage credits a player with all ways of reaching base and extending an inning, e.g. walks, hit by pitch, etc. What the Oakland A's figured out, and what Michael Lewis reported in his book, is that the cost of a high-batting-average player was out of line with the cost of a low-batting-average player who had a high on base percentage. The A's also discovered that players with low batting averages but good on base percentages were more available than players with high batting averages.

A collection of players with high on base percentages would delay outs, extend innings, put more pressure on opposing pitchers, push more players around the bases, score more runs and, ultimately, win more games. This is elementary, and yet professional baseball organizations obsessed with batting averages had ignored the principle. Every Little League coach tells his players that "A walk is as good as a hit," but they say that to the kids they don't want swinging the bat. By the time Major League scouts evaluate players, the humble bromide is completely forgotten.

Despite working with a shoestring budget, the A's became a competitive franchise by employing players most other franchises found unexciting. Nonetheless, there were doubts in the minds of the "experts" because the A's didn't look as good as their record. They didn't pass the exalted "eyeball test." (This should sound like an echo from the 2003 Badgers basketball team.) While opposing players flew around the bases after hits, the A's players more often moved station to station after walks. But the wins piled up, and the A's paid less per victory than their opponents. Soon other franchises employed nerds to parse the numbers and find secrets and advantages that had been overlooked by hidebound experts for decades. If it could happen in baseball, couldn't it happen in basketball, a game adorned with relatively few statistics?

Moneyball for Basketball

The analogy to basketball is apt. Baseball scouts look first for physical skills—hitting, running, and throwing—and often ignore less eye-catching skills, like managing the strike zone and not wasting at bats. Basketball recruiters also look for physical skills—impressive dunking, harrowing drives to the basket, and body-bruising rebounding—and often ignore less eye-catching skills, like ball handling, passing, shooting, and decision making. But are the fundamental basketball skills the keys to winning games—as they are in baseball—and can those keys be distilled into a new set of statistics?

This brings us back to that game long ago between the Badgers and the Spartans. If the Badgers won by factors obscured by traditional box score statistics, if new statistics are needed to explain the outcome of games, then the black swan could not have been a singular event. Over the next thirteen years, I examined thousands of box scores and found hundreds of black swan games. In these games, the winner trailed in field goal shooting percentage and total rebounds, or the loser led in both categories. Not only were black swans not a rarity, but traditional box score statistics had to be considered unreliable measures of team quality. Just as for baseball, traditional basketball statistics undervalued factors that led to victories. As a result, teams that didn't pass the eyeball test were undervalued despite their successes on the court.

This is the first reason why it is so difficult to pick winners in the NCAA Tournament bracket: *We tend to pick teams that look good on the court, and we tend to pick teams with glowing box score statistics.*

For thirteen years, I've waited for game announcers and color analysts to stop talking about field goal percentage and total rebounds, but they still try to explain games using those unreliable statistics. For thirteen years, I've waited for the purveyors of advanced analytics to stumble upon the simple truths in this book, but I'm not aware of any who have. Instead, one highly publicized service offers to discover whether teams are more competitive during final exams or when the star player's mother is in attendance. Interesting information, but not deterministic analytics.

To make the arguments that follow more digestible, I've used a sample of forty-seven teams from the 2017-2018 basketball season. These teams were seeded one through six in the tournament bracket (the experts' picks as the best twenty-four teams in the country) plus twenty-three other teams that either were ranked by the polls during the season or were embroiled in controversies over tournament selection and seeding. Arguably, these were the forty-seven best teams of the season. These teams played a total of 1,659 games to produce a statistically valid sample.

More importantly, field goal percentage and total rebounds are just two of the statistics currently in use that may be unreliable in explaining basketball outcomes. We have yet to examine free throws, turnovers, offensive rebounds, assists, and fouls, to name a few.

Distorted Inputs

However, unreliable statistics are but one input we consider when making our tournament bracket selections. As we'll see in later chapters, new statistics will clarify our evaluation of teams, but we will continue to absorb information from other sources too.

The most natural way to evaluate teams: Watch the games and form subjective opinions. The media refers to this method as the "eyeball test." Thanks to cable and satellite television, most fans have access to more basketball games than they have time to watch. Fans and experts believe they can judge whether one or both teams played well simply by watching them play. The reliance on the eyeball test leaves me as queasy as I would be if my physician were to tell me that since I look healthy I needn't worry about my blackouts or the numbness in my left arm. Typically, fans assign too much credit to dunks, fast breaks, and derring-do drives to the "hole." Typically, fans assign too much credit to offense and not enough to defense. And they assign more credit to a team that plays at a fast pace and not enough to teams that play slower. Games played at a fast pace with a high offensive output based upon drives, dunks, and fast breaks please the eye.

The heralded eyeball test fails in another critical dimension: It is virtually impossible for any viewer, whether fan or expert, to adjust his evaluation of team performance based upon the strength of the opponent. A good performance leaves an indelible impression on the brain whether the opponent was strong or weak. The reverse is true as well.

The corollary is that the eyeball test fails to discriminate between team A's good performance against team B, and team C's good performance against team D. Which was the better performance and by exactly how much? For this we need objective statistics to override subjective evaluation.

The undeniable conclusion: Watching games is entertainment, but it is not suitable for comparative evaluation. *Do not pick teams because you think they look good on TV.*

So the second option we have for judging basketball teams is to listen to the experts and accept their opinions. However, it is difficult to find unadulterated information about sports. Virtually all broadcast sports content is a mixture of showmanship, opinion, slanted salesmanship, and a few selected facts. When we hear expert opinions, we should remember that the first job of a broadcast expert is to entertain viewers, the second job is to sell advertising time, the third job is to pump up future viewing events, and way down at number four is the job of sharing their expertise.

Experts suffer from the ingestion of the same distorted inputs as do fans. Worse, experts suffer from inbred, inside-the-box thinking based upon a lifetime of living inside the game. What the experts learned at the age of six has become as true for them today as the sun rising in the East and setting in the West. They cling to the past like a shipwrecked man clings to a raft. If one were to track their predictions in games between comparable teams, one would find that they are no more accurate than flipping a coin.

If you listened to the experts this year, you may have drunk the Arizona Kool-Aid and blown up your bracket on day one. You might have chosen Duke, or Michigan State to win the tournament, Virginia or North Carolina to reach the Final Four. And you'd never have picked Loyola (Chicago) to reach the Final Four.

You Are What Your Record Says You Are

A famous professional football coach has said it's so. Of course, he's talking about an organized league where schedules, the draft, and payroll rules are designed to level the playing field. Such is not the case in college basketball. Some schools have, and exploit, greater resources than others. Schedules are unequal. Recruiting classes and talent levels vary widely. Nonetheless, computer systems and ranking polls intuit cosmic meaning from wins and losses. As a fan fills the tournament bracket, the temptation to favor teams with better won/lost records, better head-to-head results, more good wins, or fewer bad losses, will be irresistible. Throw in conference championships, especially conference tournament championships, and you have the foul-smelling slop you would never eat for lunch.

America's obsession with winning ranks near the top of a list that includes sex, celebrities, scandals, automobiles, and money. In the public perception, winning is good, losing is bad, and there isn't anything very complicated about the matter. Winning is the only object of the games we play, so it seems eminently logical to gauge the quality of a team by the size of the number in its win column.

As unassailable as this statement seems to be, it is, nonetheless, the logic that sparks the controversy surrounding the tournament selection committee and fuels debate over the polls. This faulty logic causes the arguments between you and your neighbor over the backyard fence.

"Win" and "lose" are like pass or fail grades on a test in school; they are binary summaries of complex events, and much information is lost in the summation. Take, for example, a situation in which four students score ninety-nine, seventy-one, sixty-nine, and twenty-nine on the same math test. If the test is graded on a pass/fail basis with a score of seventy being the minimum requirement to pass, two students fail the test and two students pass. As a result, the passing scores of ninety-nine and seventy-one become equivalent and the failing scores of sixty-nine and twenty-nine become equivalent, but the gulf between the seventy-one and the sixty-nine is as wide as the Grand Canyon.

Clearly these four students exhibit widely divergent degrees of mathematical competence (a quantitative measure), but that is not apparent if all that is visible are two "passes" and two "fails" (binary measures). "W" and "L" expose the same amount of information as "pass" and "fail," and they also conceal the same amount of information. If we want to know how well these four students know math, we wouldn't limit our investigation to whether they passed or failed the test. We would examine the actual test scores to obtain an accurate assessment. The same is true when comparing wins and losses for basketball teams.

The undisputable fact is that a team can play poorly and still win a basketball game (pass a test) if its opponent plays worse. We've all witnessed games in which a team won "ugly," games in which neither team could "get anything going." As binary statistics, won/lost records treat all wins equally, thus the team that wins "ugly" receives no less credit than the team that dazzles us with its scintillating performance. Duke received no less credit for stinking up the gym against Southern University and South Dakota than it did for dismantling Michigan State in non-conference play. Conversely, a team can play well and yet lose if its opponent plays marginally better. Duke received no more credit for playing very well in a loss to North Carolina, than it did for playing terribly in a loss to North Carolina State.

Rather than illuminating and enlightening, won/lost records obfuscate, conceal information, and deceive fans and experts alike. Records obscure qualitative measures in the same way that my golf scorecard concealed the way I completed my round last weekend. After hitting my tee shot into the trees, I punched out onto the fairway and then topped a "worm-burner" that skidded to within sixty yards of the green. The golf gods then blessed me with a once-in-a-lifetime pitch shot that staggered all over the green before dropping in the cup for a par four. My buddies congratulated me by saying, "There are no pictures on a scorecard." There are no pictures on a won/lost record either.

When used appropriately, won/lost records can simplify various decisions that arise in sports. For example, seeding in conference tournaments can be based upon regular season records. In conferences that have round-robin scheduling, conference won/lost records can determine the conference champion. Unfortunately, the Big 12 is the only power conference that schedules home-and-home games against all members of the conference and is, therefore, the only power conference in which a true regular season champion can be crowned. In the other five power conferences, the luck of the scheduling draw can unfairly favor one team over another in any season. This season, Virginia played Duke and North Carolina once each, while those teams played each other twice.

Ironically, the polls and computers look at the problem from the opposite angle and attempt to deduce meaning from wins and losses, like an astronomer searching for stars by looking into an observatory through the large end of the telescope.

Winning doesn't automatically mean that a team is "good"; it simply means that the winning team played *relatively* better than the losing team, on game day, under a certain set of circumstances. Therefore, winning and losing are relative measures and not definitive or decisive events. If the circumstances were changed or if the teams played a second time, (or, if there were different referees in some of this year's tournament games), the outcome could well be different.

Won/lost records are merely the sum of pass/ fail results for some number of tests without any qualifying information about the difficulty of the tests or the grades achieved on the tests. A student isn't well-educated simply because she passes tests; a student passes the tests because she is well-educated.

The same can be said of college basketball teams: *A team isn't good because it wins. A team wins because it is good.*

Chapter Three
The Missing Ingredients

Ignorance is preferable to error, and he is less remote from the truth who believes nothing than he who believes what is wrong.
—THOMAS JEFFERSON

We can trust that the winning team in any game deserves our respect because it has played better in some way than the losing team. The game would be a meaningless exercise if this weren't true. However, any freshman college student taking Philosophy 101 will immediately ask, "Relative to what?" The answer: Relative to an opponent of unknown quality.

This raises the interesting question of whether a team is "good" simply because its opponents are "bad," or is bad simply because its opponents are good. Winning simply means that one team played *relatively* better than the other team on game day. The winning team may not have played well enough to beat your recreation league team. Losing doesn't automatically mean that a team is bad either. Losing simply means that one team played *relatively* less well than the other team played. In every contest, one team plays *relatively* better than the other.

Immediately, we are faced with two problems: 1) we don't how "good" the winning team's opponent happened to be, and 2) we don't have a precise measurement of how well either team played in this game.

To find a precise measurement of playing performance, we would naturally look to currently available statistics, most readily available in the venerable box score. The box score, we find, is a collection of individual player effort measures that are summed to represent team effort. As any good businessman knows, it is a mistake to reward effort when results are the keys to success. As any good statistical analyst knows, statistics that measure effort are useless in the absence of statistics that determine results. Since we don't have deterministic statistics, we don't know how good any one team is and we don't know how good any opponent is.

This seemingly intractable problem is largely ignored by poll voters who make guesses each week and by experts who feign confidence in knowing the unknowable.

Garbage In, Garbage Out

To the rescue comes the Rating Percentage Index, better known as the RPI. This method has been declared dead and buried on more than one occasion, but its ghost haunts college basketball like a specter in a horror movie.

Invented originally as a coarse measure of schedule strength, the RPI answers a question with questions, solves a riddle with more riddles, and mathematically deduces the solution to an equation with no known values. In the Information Technology industry, it is known as garbage in, garbage out, or GIGO. It is the tenet that the output from a computer system or mathematical algorithm is only as good as the input.

RPI attempts to calculate the strength of Team A, an admitted unknown, by first calculating its winning percentage (wins divided by total games played) and giving that number, a number for which it is trying to determine a value, a weight of 25% in its algorithm. So, we start with the unknown value we are attempting to solve for as part of the answer. That won't produce a definitive answer.

Since RPI doesn't know the value of Team A's record, it calculates the winning percentage of its opponents by summing all wins and dividing by all games played. Now, the value of each of those won/lost records is just as unknown as the value of Team A's won/lost record (in fact, RPI will go through the same illogical process with each of those teams) but Team A's Opponents' winning percentage is given a weight of 50% and added to Team A's winning percentage. So, now we have Team A's unknown value added to thirty or more other unknown values and we haven't solved for anything yet (in the mathematical sense).

Step three is to calculate the winning percentages for all of Team A's opponents' opponents' won/lost records, give them a weight of 25%, and add those hundreds of unknown values to the ~31 unknown values we already had in the algorithm.

We still don't have a single known or absolute value in the calculation but that's it: a string of unknown values is thrown together in an abominable stew to produce a meaningless number that will mislead selection committee members as they seed the brackets and sports fans as they fill their March Madness™ brackets.

A mathematician would represent the RPI formula as:

$$A = (.25X) + (.5*{\sim}30Y) + (.25*{\sim}900Z)$$

where A is the value of the team for which we are calculating a value, X equals the value of the team's record, Y equals the value of its opponents' records, and Z equals the value of its opponents' opponents' records. Since X and Y and Z are all unknown, A must also be unknown.

Although the formula can be represented with mathematical notation, the RPI method is flawed because you can't solve for an unknown value using only unknown values, and every won/lost record is an unknown value.

College basketball teams play within a conference and share with their rivals most of the same conference opponents. Within a conference, the poorest teams will have the best opponent records (those of the teams in the conference that finished ahead of them in the standings), and the best teams in the conference will have the weakest opponent records (the records of their weaker conference foes). Obviously, this logic is upside-down and shifts the burden of differentiation of the better teams to nonconference opponents.

RPI also discounts home victories and road losses while penalizing home losses and rewarding road wins. While this approach may seem logical at first blush, its application can produce unintended results. Since power conference schools play virtually all nonconference games at home while nonpower conference teams are forced to play many nonconference games on the road, and since power conference teams typically schedule weaker teams in preseason while their opponents tend to play teams stronger than themselves, a nonpower school record can and often does have more value than an identical power conference record.

All records are not equal, until they get combined in an RPI rating.

House of Cards

The danger is that the NCAA Men's Basketball Committee, the august group that determines tournament selections and seeds, uses the RPI indirectly to assess "good" wins and "bad" losses. This year the committee invented something it calls the quadrant system. The committee divided the 351 Division I basketball teams into four quadrants based upon their (illogical and misleading) RPI ratings and game locations (home, away and neutral site). Wins against quadrant I teams were considered good; losses against quadrant four teams were considered bad. Presumably wins against quadrant II are pretty good and losses against quadrant III are pretty bad.

The obvious question would be: What is the science behind the subdivisions? Is it anything more than a guess?

The Missing Ingredients

Clearly, an accurate method of ranking teams requires an accurate measure of team playing performance and an accurate measure of opponent strength. Only then will fans have the most important inputs they need to pick tournament bracket winners.

Chapter Four

Geek Numbers

*We are drowning in information but
starved for knowledge.*
—JOHN NAISBITT

The definition of a "good" team begins with one simple concept: *Good teams play well.* To measure playing performance, we will have to invent new statistics that are deterministic—that is, statistics that determine the outcome of games. The better a team performs in these categories, the more victories it will produce. Even in losses, these new statistics will measure playing performance and assign the correct credit for the loser's effort.

Repair and Replace

The raw materials for deterministic statistics already exist in the traditional box score. The measurements simply must be modified to be useful. The traditional box score records the following information:

1. Field goals attempted (both two-pointers and three-pointers)
2. Field goals made (both two-pointers and three-pointers)
3. Field goal percentage (gross percentage, a statistic that causes black swans)
4. Three-point field goals attempted
5. Three-point field goals made
6. Three-point field goal percentage
7. Free throws attempted
8. Free throws made
9. Free throw percentage
10. Defensive rebounds
11. Offensive rebounds
12. Total rebounds (the other statistic that causes black swans)
13. Turnovers

14. Assists
15. Fouls committed

We'll begin by correcting three of these statistics.

Field Goal Percentage

The traditional field goal percentage statistic lumps two-point attempts, three-point attempts, and two-pointers made and three-pointers made into a single statistic as though all attempts and all makes were equal. They are not. Three-point baskets are fifty percent more valuable. The traditional field goal percentage statistic is useless and misleading when measuring playing performance because it doesn't credit teams for their ability to score additional points with three-point blasts.

The correct calculation of field goal percentage, a statistic I call *Effective Shooting Percentage*, is:

((points scored – free throws made) / 2) / field goals attempted

This calculation turns each three-pointer made into one and a half two-pointers made (which is their effect) and produces a percentage that accurately reflects the *effectiveness* of field goal shooting. Effective Shooting Percentage relates directly to points scored, and points scored relate to victories produced.

Rebounds

The total rebound statistic is misleading—and causes black swans—because it favors teams that allow excessive shots on goal and therefore grab an excessive number of defensive rebounds. It also penalizes teams that shoot well and therefore have few offensive rebounding opportunities.

The correct rebounding statistic should reward teams for grabbing the most rebounds *available* under each basket. The correct calculation is:

(defensive rebounds / (defensive rebounds + opponent offensive rebounds)) + (offensive rebounds / (offensive rebounds + opponent defensive rebounds))

This calculation identifies the team that grabbed the most rebounds *available* under each basket. We can simply call this the *Available Rebounding Percentage* statistic.

Assists

At some point in the deep, dark past, someone decided to compare assists to turnovers to measure the effectiveness of point guard play. Since this is an individual statistic and not a team statistic, and since assists and turnovers bear no relationship to one another, I've discarded it as not useful. However, the relationship between assists and field goals made, reveals how difficult a team is to defend. The higher the assist-to-field-goals-made ratio, the more difficult a team is to defend. If you don't believe it, think back to the Pete Carril-coached Princeton teams that shocked fans with tournament upsets of heralded major conference teams. The correct calculation of the assists statistic is:

team assists / field goals made

This statistic, which I call the *Assists-to-Baskets Ratio*, produces a measure of teamwork.

A Test of Validity

When field goal percentage and rebounds are properly calculated, the number of unexplainable black swans is reduced dramatically. That tells us we are on the right track in creating new statistics because the correct statistics will explain the outcome of every game.

However, percentages may have been the culprits Mark Twain had in mind when he said, "There are lies, damned lies and statistics." When the Effective Shooting Percentages of two teams are compared after a game, they can lie to us because the number of field goal attempts may be wildly different for the two teams. In many black swan games, the winner had a lower Effective Shooting Percentage than the loser but still scored more points from the floor because they took more shots from the floor. For example, Virginia edged Boston College despite having a lower Effective Shooting Percentage (and traditional shooting percentage), because its percentage was earned on six more shots from the floor. Virginia actually outscored Boston College by four points from the floor. The final margin of victory was a single point, so floor shooting was the determining factor in the outcome and the game wasn't a black swan.

To prevent a percentage from lying, I adjust Effective Shooting Percentage for the number of shots taken from the floor and for the relative quality of the percentage. The average Effective Shooting Percentage for the twenty sample teams and their opponents was 54.2 percent, and the average number of shots from the floor per game was 58.9. Thus, the modified calculation of floor shooting performance becomes:

(effective shooting percentage / .542)
X (field goals attempted / 58.9)

This calculation rewards teams for shooting better than average, penalizes teams for shooting worse than average, and calibrates for differences in the numbers of shots taken.

We're Not Done Yet

To eliminate the remaining black swans, explain all game outcomes, and comparatively rank team playing performances, two more measures of playing performance must be invented and combined with Effective Shooting Percentage and Available Rebounding Percentage.

The Importance of Empty Possessions

As we saw in the Wisconsin/Michigan State black swan game, the excessive number of turnovers Michigan State committed provided Wisconsin with more chances to score, and that allowed Wisconsin to shoot poorly and yet score the same number of points from the floor. In addition to turnovers, offensive rebounds impact possessions by adding chances to score. So we need a statistic that combines turnovers and offensive rebounds in a way that identifies the team that produced the most chances to score. The following equation calculates a team's additional *Chances to Score*:

(offensive rebounds + opponent's turnovers) – (turnovers + opponent's offensive rebounds)

While this statistic produces a raw number of chances to score over and above the number of equal possessions in any game, it does not gauge the importance of the number relative to a specific game's possessions. Unlike baseball, there is no prescribed number of possessions in a basketball game. Some teams play fast— Auburn and Florida State averaged nearly seventy-four possessions per game—while others play slow— Virginia averaged only sixty-one possessions per game. Using the average number of possessions in the games played by the forty-seven sample teams this season—a little more than seventy (70.21)—we can accurately gauge the impact of the additional Chances to Score:

chances to score / 70.21

When combined with Effective Shooting Percentage and the properly calculated Available

Rebounding statistic, Chances to Score eliminates the Wisconsin/Michigan State game from the list of unexplainable black swans.

Don't Bring a Knife to a Gunfight

Although TV highlights focus on dunks, fast breaks, and drives to the hoop, those two-point baskets are like knives in a gunfight. Not only are they more difficult to produce than free throws, they are also far less potent in adding points to the scoreboard than are three-point baskets. A team that shoots 33.3 percent from the three-point arc scores as many points as a team that shoots 50 percent from inside the arc, but this mathematical fact is as easily overlooked by basketball experts as walks were overlooked by baseball experts.

We can eliminate the last of our black swan games by inventing a statistic that combines the impact of easy points scored at the aptly named "charity" stripe, with the nuclear power of three-point baskets. I call this the *Easy Points Mix* and it looks like this:

points scored / (field goals attempted + (free throws attempted / 2))

This statistic reflects the impact of three-pointers and easy free throws on the scoreboard. The average three-point shooting percentage for the sample teams during the 2017-2018 season was 37.24 percent and their two-point shooting percentage was 53.16 percent, meaning the teams scored more points by attempting threes than by attempting twos. However, the average number of three-point attempts per game was only 22.4 as compared to 37.16 two-point attempts per game. Strategically thinking, that makes no sense. The sample teams averaged 72.85 percent from the free throw on an average of only 19.8 attempts per game.

When this calculation is combined with the other four properly calculated metrics, all game outcomes are explained statistically, and all black swans are eliminated.

The Five Measures of Playing Performance

The following five metrics accurately describe every college basketball game in mathematical terms:

1. Effective Shooting Percentage
2. Available Rebounding Percentage
3. Assists-to-Baskets Ratio
4. Chances to Score, and
5. Easy Points Mix

These five statistics determine all outcomes, explain all outcomes, eliminate black swans, and accurately measure the playing performance of college basketball teams. We now know that all swans are white and that some appeared to be black only because faulty statistics were used to explain the outcomes. In every game, the winner played better in some dimension than the loser.

Adding Weight to the Five Performance Metrics

Before the forty-seven sample teams can be ranked, the performance metrics must be assigned a relative weight in the calculation. The metrics vary in their importance to winning basketball games based upon how often teams won when exceeding losers in each statistical category, how often teams lost while trailing in the category, and how often teams led opponents in each category. The following table depicts the impact of each metric:

METRIC	WIN % SUPERIOR GRADE	WIN % INFERIOR GRADE	FREQUENCY OF SUPERIOR GRADE
Effective Shooting %	92.93%	32.75%	69.84%
Easy Points Mix	93.88%	32.00%	69.14%
Available Rebounding %	78.72%	67.95%	63.40%
Assists-to-Baskets Ratio	81.64%	67.94%	64.87%
Chances to Score	77.56%	70.85%	58.55%

In the playing performance algorithm, Effective Shooting Percentage and Easy Points Mix have a weight of 30% each; Available Rebounding Percentage and Assists-to-Baskets

Ratio have a weight of 15% each; and, Chances to Score has a weight of 10%.

A Note about Shooting Percentages

Effective Shooting Percentage and Easy Points Mix allow sportscasters and color analysts to communicate game analysis effectively to fans. In the calculation of playing performance grades, both metrics are calculated for offense and defense (opponent's metrics). Available Rebounding Percentage and Chances to Score inherently incorporate both offense and defense. Assists-to-Baskets ratio applies to each team individually.

If fans can identify the teams that are best at these five categories of playing performance, they can intelligently fill out their tournament brackets.

A Note about playing Styles

These accurate analytics should influence playing styles. The numbers argue for careful play to limit turnovers and aggressive offensive rebounding to increase opportunities to score. The numbers argue for recruiting shooters first because free throws are the easiest points to score and three-point baskets are the most powerful baskets to make. Loyola's success was based upon cutting, passing, assisting, and shooting. Villanova won this year's tournament because their players could shoot the ball.

Counterintuitively, most coaches recruit great athletes who can dribble-drive and dunk. The sample teams averaged only twenty-two three-point attempts per game (37.6 percent of shots from the floor). The sample teams scored only 31.7 percent of their points from beyond the arc while shooting 37.24 percent. Sample teams scored only 18.3 percent of their points from the free throw line while shooting a pedestrian average.

The sample teams scored 50 percent of their points on two-point baskets—the vast majority of them dunks and lay-ins. Since even good teams are over reliant on pick-and-roll plays, crossover dribbles and alley-oops, the numbers argue for a defense that allows three-point attempts and limits the dribble-drive. There is such a defense, the pack line defense employed successfully by Virginia (and a few others). Alternatively, coaches could play a zone defense that forces opponents to move without the ball and pass crisply, skills most opponents do not possess.

Chapter Five

Circumstantial Evidence

Everything is relative in this world …
—**LEON TROTSKY**

"Relative to what?" The question of the freshman philosophy student rings loudly in the background as we attempt to measure team playing performance. We know instinctively that not all wins are equal and neither are all losses. A victory over an Atlantic Coast Conference (ACC) team generally carries more weight than a victory over a team from Conference USA, but Middle Tennessee would be an exception to that generalization. Where would that very good team rank relative to all ACC teams? And how can we distinguish between an ACC team and a team from another power conference?

We hear the experts talk of "good wins" and "bad losses," but it isn't enough to single out a game here and there. Team rankings require that every playing performance grade be adjusted to reflect the strength of the opponent. The definition of a "good" team can be expanded to include this principle: *Good teams play well against opponents that play well.*

Thus, we face the insoluble problem of Strength of Schedule (SOS). We've already discredited won/lost records, which aren't adjusted for SOS in any event. We've already discredited the RPI, which is based upon discredited won/lost records. So what are we to do?

An Imperfect Solution

Strictly speaking, no one knows how good any team is on opening day of basketball season, yet many preseason polls are published. As teams lose, they drop a few positions in the rankings, and winners backfill the available slots. The voters repeat this mechanical process every week until we reach the end of the regular season. At that point, an all-powerful committee decides which teams will be invited to the tournament and how they will be seeded in the tournament field.

Although imperfect, the polls provide a controlled environment within which to apply our accurately composed statistical equations. However, I didn't adopt any one poll as the definitive source of SOS input. Taking the approach millennials have taught us so well, I used the wisdom of the masses to gauge the relative strength of each team.

The wisdom of the masses is embodied in the Massey College Basketball Ranking Composite, which homogenizes fifty-five ranking opinions into a single ranked list of the three hundred fifty-one major college basketball teams. The list can be found online at http://www.mratings. com/cb/compare.htm. Even then, I allowed for significant error. I grouped the teams into seven scientifically defined categories and assigned the same SOS factor to all teams within a category. In this way, I accounted for voter error of anywhere from twenty-five to fifty positions within the ranking list. The categories are as follows:

1. Elite teams ranked 1-12
2. Very good teams ranked 13-37
3. Highly competitive teams ranked 38-75
4. Competitive teams ranked 76-100
5. Average teams ranked 101-150
6. Weak teams ranked 151-250
7. Very weak teams ranked 251-351

Games against very weak teams were assigned an SOS value of 1.0, meaning the playing performance grade was unadjusted and a "W" was simply a "W." In wins against teams in higher categories, playing performance grades were incremented according to precisely how much more difficult it was for the sample teams to defeat teams in that category. Unlike the committee's arbitrary quadrants, our SOS categories were based upon actual game results and the playing performance adjustments were based upon the strength differences between the categories.

Playing performance grades were decremented for losses. A loss to an Elite Team was given an adjustment value of 1.0, meaning an "L" was just an "L." Losses to teams in lower categories were penalized based upon the difficulty of playing teams in each category. For the sample teams, playing performance scores were consistent for each category which proved the validity of this approach.

Home Cooking

One final adjustment was made to the SOS factor to account for home court advantage. When playing at home, SOS factors were unadjusted, but when playing on the road, the SOS factor was incremented by 7 percent to account for the fact that playing performance grades were 7 percent better on average when teams played at home. This adjustment levels the playing field and turns all games into the equivalent of home games.

Comparative SOS

The full season schedules of the top thirty-two sample teams ranked as follows:

1. 118.32 – Kansas
2. 118.12 – North Carolina
3. 118.01 – Oklahoma
4. 117.77 – Kentucky
5. 117.73 – Florida
6. 117.60 – Texas A&M
7. 117.43 – Butler
8. 117.42 – Villanova
9. 117.41 – Texas Tech
10. 117.41 – Duke
11. 117.35 – Tennessee
12. 117.27 – West Virginia
13. 117.21 – TCU
14. 116.98 – Clemson
15. 116.61 – Xavier
16. 116.09 – Creighton
17. 115.99 – Ohio State
18. 115.94 – Miami
19. 115.91 – Michigan
20. 115.76 – Purdue

21. 115.66 – Virginia
22. 115.61 – Auburn
23. 115.08 – Arizona State
24. 114.92 – Arizona
25. 114.41 – Michigan State
26. 114.39 – Wichita State
27. 114.10 – Nevada
28. 114.02 – Houston
29. 113.94 – Rhode Island
30. 113.76 – Cincinnati
31. 112.64 – Gonzaga
32. 111.45 – Saint Mary's

Apparent from this comparative list, the Big 12 and Southeastern Conference (SEC) teams played far more difficult schedules than did Pac-12 teams. Pac-12 teams may have been overrated when applying the eyeball test and may have been picked on tournament brackets when they shouldn't have been (Pac-12 teams failed to win even a single game in this year's tournament). Also interesting is the confirming fact that teams from the non-Power Six conferences did play easier schedules.

However, what must be noted is that difference from top to bottom is not as great as experts and committee members might think. This year the difference between the very best teams and the very weakest teams has shrunk to just 13.9% of playing performance grades. The committee members wouldn't have known this fact as they arbitrarily assigned "good" to some wins and "bad" to some losses. The wins weren't as good as they thought; and the losses weren't as bad.

The Complete Algorithm

We now have a complete, final algorithm for grading the playing performances of college basketball teams. It looks like this:

(offensive grade + defensive grade) X location adjustment factor X SOS factor

This algorithm produces a grade for the playing performance of both teams in any game. Game grades are then summed and averaged for the number of games played to produce a seasonal grade.

Chapter Six

Relative Performance Grading

We judge ourselves by what we feel capable of doing, while others judge us by what we have already done.
—HENRY WADSWORTH LONGFELLOW

I've named the collection of five performance metrics, the SOS factor and the home court factor the Relative Performance Grading System, or RPG for short. A ranking system is distinguished from voting polls by its philosophy and the rules to which it adheres. On the other hand, the diverse individual philosophies of hundreds of voters characterize voting polls, and that's one reason they are useless. The RPG system adheres to a short list of simple rules:

1. Full Body of Work

    Every game is graded and every game carries the same weight. Poll voters and fans tend to forget games that are more than two weeks in the past. As a result, all wins become equal and all losses become equal in their short-term memories.

2. Flat-footed Start

    All teams begin the season without a grade and then earn grades for performance in real games. No preseason poll positions teams before they accomplish anything. No expert guesses corrupt actual performance. Teams that get off to a slow start, as Baylor and Villanova did this season, do not get credit for potential. They will be ranked low until they build a resume of good playing performances.

3. Head-to-Head Results Have No Intrinsic Importance

Fans are sometimes confused when their favorite team is ranked behind a rival it defeated.

4. Late Season Games Are Not More Important than Early Season Games

Unlike football teams that follow a smooth trajectory, either improving or declining over the course of a season, basketball teams ride a roller coaster of wrenching ups and downs.

5. SOS Is Based upon Final Polls

Some voters argue that game-day rankings are more important than final rankings. They claim a psychological effect is at work when playing highly ranked teams, even if those teams later prove themselves to be also-rans. Since the same voters cause these mistaken rankings, we can dismiss this approach as self-apologetic. If team grades are to be based upon a full body of work, SOS grades must also be based upon a full body of work.

6. RPG Grades Replace Wins and Losses

Won/lost records are not included in any RPG calculation. When a team outplays its opponent (and wins the game), it receives a higher grade than its opponent. When a team is outplayed by its opponent (and loses the game), it receives a lower grade than its opponent. In all games, both teams are graded for performance and neither team receives a misleading "W" or "L" to conceal the quality of its play. As a result, Michigan State received more credit—a better grade— for its shocking loss to Syracuse than it did for its lackluster performance in a win over Illinois during conference play. Similarly, Alabama graded better in its loss to Texas A&M than it did in a victory over UT Arlington. Won/lost records sway fans to make the wrong picks when filling their tournament brackets.

Read 'em and Weep

The box score statistics for regular season games, including conference tournament games, were pumped into the RPG formula to rank teams prior to the NCAA Tournament. The selection committee should have used this definitive ranking to seed teams in the tournament field. This could have been the most valuable input for fans in picking winners on their tournament bracket. The following table lists the teams in ranked order and identifies the seed each team should have earned.

RPG RANKINGS END OF REGULAR SEASON				
RPG RANK	TEAM	RPG GRADE	NCAA SEED	RPG SEED
1	Virginia	112.74	1	1
2	Villanova	111.85	1	1
3	Duke	111.29	2	1
4	Cincinnati	111.22	2	1
5	Michigan State	110.49	3	2
6	North Carolina	109.86	2	2
7	Purdue	107.65	2	2
8	Gonzaga	107.60	4	2
9	Wichita State	107.39	4	3
10	Xavier	106.68	1	3
11	Kansas	106.57	1	3
12	Tennessee	105.87	3	3
13	Michigan	105.81	3	4
14	Houston	104.88	6	4
15	Nevada	104.68	7	4
16	Auburn	104.33	4	4
17	Arizona	103.92	4	5
18	St. Mary's	103.78	None	5

19	West Virginia	103.44	5	5
20	Texas Tech	103.05	3	5
21	Ohio State	102.23	5	6
22	Rhode Island	102.14	7	6
23	Kentucky	101.96	5	6
24	TCU	101.93	6	6
25	Loyola	101.29	11	7
26	Florida	101.08	6	7
27	Middle Tennessee State	101.07	None	7
28	USC	100.85	None	7
29	Texas A&M	100.48	7	8
30	Clemson	100.46	5	8
31	Seton Hall	100.37	8	8
32	Miami	99.86	6	8
33	Arkansas	99.81	7	9
34	NC State	99.60	9	9
35	Florida State	99.37	9	9
36	Creighton	99.11	8	9
37	Arizona State	98.76	11	10
38	Virginia Tech	97.78	8	10
39	Missouri	97.50	8	10
40	Butler	97.43	10	10
41	Louisville	97.14	None	11
42	Syracuse	97.03	11	11
43	Providence	96.86	10	11
44	Kansas State	96.81	9	11
45	Oklahoma State	96.63	None	None
46	Oklahoma	96.09	10	None
47	Alabama	94.30	9	None

This year the committee made its biggest mistake in its selections to the tournament field. You might think with sixty-eight available slots they couldn't miss top twenty teams, but they did. First, the controversy over whether to invite Oklahoma or Oklahoma State was unnecessary since neither team should have been invited. Alabama also received an invite it did not deserve. Alabama finished forty-seventh in our rankings and they probably didn't deserve to be ranked that high. There was room for more teams we didn't rank to finish above them.

Conversely, Saint Mary's, Middle Tennessee State and USC deserved spots in the field with excellent seeds at No. 5, No. 7, and another No. 7, respectively. In other words, the committee mistakenly awarded twenty-three at-large bids ahead of Saint Mary's and eighteen ahead of Middle Tennessee State and USC. The answer to the earlier question about where a mid-major would fit into a Power Six conference is: Middle Tennessee State would have been the second-best team in the Pac-12 conference.

Despite its unlikely run to the Elite Eight, Kansas State was the committee's third selection mistake (along with Oklahoma and Alabama).

The committee also made a few impactful mistakes in seeding. Neither Xavier nor Kansas deserved a No. 1 seed. Both should have been No. 3 seeds, opening the door for more deserving Cincinnati and Duke to claim top spots. The built-in bias against mid-majors also deprived Gonzaga (No. 4 but should have been a No. 2), Houston (No. 6 but should have been a No. 4), Nevada (No. 7 but should have been a No. 4) and Loyola (Chicago) (No. 11 but should have been a No. 7) of seeds commensurate with their outstanding play throughout the season. That the committee made seeding mistakes on mid-major teams comes as no surprise. The committee has no scientific method to evaluate mid-major teams because there are few comparison points or games played against mythical Quadrant One teams.

As we'll discuss in a later chapter, accurate seeding isn't a matter of prestige. Inaccurate seeding changes matchups and, therefore, changes the outcome of the tournament.

Final Grades

When the music stopped and the Big Dance ended, Villanova walked off the floor with the trophy. However, they are ranked No. 1 in the RPG list not because they won the tournament, but because they turned in the best grades for the full body of 2017-2018 work. In some final polls, Michigan was ranked #2 simply because they reached the national championship game. Had the Wolverines won the tournament, those polls would have ranked Michigan No. 1. In the RPG rankings, Michigan's six tournament games were graded like all other games and averaged with all other grades. That would have been the case whether they won the title game or not.

After its dramatic run to the Final Four, Loyola (Chicago) was ranked No. 7 by one popularity poll. Of course, that poll hadn't cast even a single vote for the Ramblers before the tournament. The RPG system had Loyola at No. 25 before the tournament—the system knew they were good—and No. 28 after the tournament. Although they won tournament games in amazing style, the Ramblers' game grades were lower in tournament games than they had been in the regular season, primarily because they played tougher competition.

Here are the final grades for this "school year."

FINAL RPG RANKINGS			
RANK	TEAM	RAW RPG	ADJUSTED RPG
1	Villanova	98.69	113.56
2	Duke	99.51	111.66
3	Virginia	97.31	111.64
4	Cincinnati	101.09	111.45
5	Michigan State	99.83	110.60
6	North Carolina	98.70	109.50
7	Purdue	96.80	107.53
8	Gonzaga	98.25	107.37
9	Kansas	94.37	107.20
10	Wichita State	98.53	107.01
11	Michigan	95.82	106.41
12	Xavier	94.36	106.17
13	Tennessee	95.43	105.93
14	Nevada	96.11	105.00
15	Houston	96.54	104.70
16	Texas Tech	94.13	104.16
17	Auburn	94.43	103.91
18	West Virginia	94.95	103.85
19	St. Mary's	96.32	103.67

20	Arizona	94.33	103.40
21	Kentucky	92.59	102.42
22	Ohio State	93.44	102.41
23	Rhode Island	94.33	102.22
24	TCU	94.23	101.79
25	Clemson	92.53	101.75
26	Florida	93.63	101.70
27	Texas A&M	93.09	101.21
28	Loyola	92.36	101.10
29	Middle Tennessee State	93.82	101.07
30	Seton Hall	93.54	100.79
31	Florida State	93.04	100.74
32	USC	93.92	100.55
33	Arkansas	91.25	99.51
34	Miami	91.86	99.50
35	NC State	92.83	99.49
36	Creighton	93.27	99.07
37	Arizona State	92.72	98.79
38	Butler	91.44	98.21
39	Syracuse	91.09	98.18
40	Oklahoma State	91.48	97.65
41	Kansas State	89.76	97.62
42	Virginia Tech	91.49	97.57
43	Missouri	90.96	97.22
44	Louisville	90.90	97.13
45	Providence	90.18	96.96
46	Oklahoma	89.73	96.34
47	Alabama	88.04	94.61

"NR" means Not Ranked

Chapter Seven
'Tis the Season to Be Jolly

There is less in this than meets the eye.
—TALLULAH BANKHEAD

Experts often quote seasonal statistics to argue for the superiority of one team over another. They are fond of scoring averages, opponents' scoring averages, turnovers per game, etc., etc., ad nauseam. In every case, the experts are wrong, and if a fan listens to them, their brackets will inevitably be busted.

First, all seasonal team statistics are like uncooked meat; they are unadjusted for SOS, and therefore, meaningless and useless.

Using points per game as the metric, Virginia (54), Cincinnati (57.5), Michigan (63.3) and Syracuse (63.8), appeared to have the best scoring defenses. However, these teams held their opponents to low scoring averages because they played slow and gave opponents fewer opportunities to score. A Virginia "game" is not the same as a Cincinnati "game" or a Duke "game." Virginia averaged 61.1 possessions per game, while Cincinnati played a bit faster at 66.5 possessions per game and Duke played faster than average at 71.5 possessions per game. Scoring averages cannot be compared when the "games" these teams played were so different in opportunities to score. When pace of play is removed from the equation and points per possession is used as the more meaningful metric for comparisons, Cincinnati was best at .865, Virginia was second at .884 and Michigan State, Purdue, Houston, Loyola (Chicago) and Texas Tech all played more efficient defense than either Michigan or Syracuse.

It comes as no surprise that Villanova was the highest scoring team this season. It averaged 86.6 points per Villanova "game", an astounding number. Villanova's average drops a bit to 85.5 points per game when pace is eliminated and the team's scoring per possession is applied to a standard game of 70.21 possessions. Villanova still topped the list for scoring but watch what happens when pace is eliminated from the seasonal average for the country's second highest scoring team—Oklahoma. The Sooners were highly regarded because they scored 84.94 points per regulation game. But, when their points per possession are applied to a game of an average number of possessions, their scoring average plummets to a pedestrian 76.56 points per game. The Sooners weren't a good offensive team; they merely played a lot of possessions inefficiently.

As for scoring, turnovers must be related to an average game of 70.21 possessions before being compared team against team. Virginia was lauded this season for turning the ball over a meager 8.53 times per game. However, when turnovers per possession are used against an average number of possessions per game, Virginia finishes third behind Nevada and Michigan. For several years, West Virginia has turned its opponents over more than any other college team. That was the case again this season as the Mountaineers turned their opponents over a remarkable 16.47 times per game and 16.19 times per average game. Rhode Island came closest to matching those numbers. Pace did, however skew one team's numbers. Michigan State appeared to turn opponents over at a poor rate of 9.97 times per game (second worst among sample teams). But when the Spartans' turnover per possession average was applied to an average possession game, the Spartans turned over opponents at a very respectable rate of 13.38 times per average game.

Raw Fish

Sushi and oysters can be eaten raw; all other seafood meals should be cooked. Seasonal statistics are not sushi or oysters. They must be cooked by the processes of SOS adjustment and pace elimination, or they may be harmful to your health. When filling a tournament bracket, fans should pay little attention to raw seasonal statistics and should completely ignore any expert advice based upon raw seasonal statistics.

Chapter Eight
Cinderella's Slipper

When somebody says, 'This is not about money, it's the principle of the thing,' it's about money.
—KIN HUBBARD

The Big Dance

As each college basketball season comes crashing to a conclusion, the NCAA throws a party as dazzling as New Year's Eve, as raucous as the Fourth of July, and as bacchanalian as Mardi Gras. The media dubbed the party "March Madness" and the name has not only stuck, it has been trademarked. March Madness™ is no gourmet dining experience for the connoisseur; it is an extravagant, all-you-can-eat buffet for the blatantly gluttonous. Sixty-eight of the most accomplished college basketball teams take the stage at thirteen sites around the country for a three-week extravaganza, and every minute of play is televised. Like students at acting class, teams are thrown together in long-anticipated, and sometimes incongruous, combinations to act out sixty-seven unscripted dramas. Some teams surprise, while others disappoint; some games confirm preconceptions, while others supply shocking results. Each game changes the calculus of the tournament, as one team is eliminated and the other team advances in a rising crescendo of emotion befitting a Beethoven symphony. For rabid fans, the three-week feast can induce the slightly guilty malaise that plagues the overindulgent. And, for the winning team, there is the listless joy of survival, like that of the last gunfighter standing in a dusty Old West street.

It's fair to say that the tournament is famously popular. About three quarters of a million fans witness it in person while more than 100 million viewers (some estimates are as high as 140 million) tune into televised games. It is estimated that the

US economy loses more than two billion dollars in productivity during the three-week extravaganza as normally industrious workers are glued to television screens. Every business in America seems to run an office pool—an estimated 70 million fans fill out brackets—so that a disinterested mail clerk or the boss's babysitter can win the pool to the chagrin of more knowledgeable fans. Each year millions of brackets are submitted to ESPN's online Tourney Challenge and untold millions of other visitors consult the "bracketology" pages of the website weeks in advance of the tournament. According to the American Gaming Association, $9.2 billion may have been gambled on the 2017 tournament.

More importantly, the tournament generates cash like teenagers grow zits. In 2016, the NCAA extended its contract with CBS Sports and Turner Broadcasting through the 2032 tournament year. The contract will pay the association $8.8 billion for the broadcast rights, an average of $550 million per year. By 2025, the NCAA will rake in more than $1 billion each year for broadcast rights alone. Most of the TV money, plus gate receipts, is divided among

NCAA member schools. While the majority of the loot is evenly divided among the thirty-one member conferences and 351 Division I schools, the formula dictates that a big chunk of the take goes to the conferences represented by the sixty-eight teams that play in the tournament. In a typical the-rich-get-richer scheme, this "performance pay" is distributed according to the number of games played by each conference. Each game played this year was worth about $1.7 million, meaning that Villanova and Michigan earned about $8.3 million in performance pay.

Self-fulfilling Prophecy

High stakes, big money, hoopla, suspense, pageantry, notoriety, and a championship decided on the court—what could possibly be wrong with such an idyllic scenario? Just one small thing: The NCAA Tournament wasn't designed to determine the best team in the country. According to the fairy tale by the Brothers Grimm, Cinderella arrived late at the ball and departed early, but left an enduring impression on the prince while she was in attendance. Her cruel stepsisters tried to trick the prince into believing they were worthy of his affections, but the prince applied a test that the stepsisters couldn't pass: Only one foot fit the golden[1] slipper, and that foot belonged to Cinderella.

The NCAA Tournament isn't constructed to identify this mythological version of Cinderella. Twenty-seven of the last twenty-nine winners have been seeded No. 3 or higher, but the winner is rarely *the* best team in the country, the mythological Cinderella. Any top three seeded team's feet will fit the NCAA's tarnished slipper.

So the media incorrectly dubs a lowly seed that wins two games and reaches the Sweet Sixteen to be "Cinderella." Using this incorrect definition, two of the last thirty-four winners qualify for the Cinderella label: No. 7 seeded Connecticut, which won the 2014 installment of the tournament; and, No. 8 seeded Villanova which won the title in 1985, the first year of expansion.

In two famous cases the Cinderella label was incorrectly applied to teams that the Committee

---

1   In the original fairy tale, Cinderella's slipper is golden, not glass. The glass slipper is a Hollywood invention.

simply seeded far lower than they deserved: George Mason in 2006; and, VCU in 2011. This year Loyola (Chicago) bore the burden of a No. 11 seed when it should have had a No. 7 seed. According to RPG, Loyola was favored against Miami (would have saved a lot of brackets), pulled mild upsets over Tennessee and Nevada, and won a game against Kansas State in which it was heavily favored.

The reasons for this sad condition are counterintuitive:

1. Few teams of any caliber are left on the sidelines by the NCAA Men's Basketball Championship Tournament Committee, and that is a characteristic that appeals to its fans.

   Proponents of the tournament format believe that if all good teams are in the field, the tournament is a fair test and the best team will magically emerge like a magician's beautiful assistant emerges unscathed after her coffin has been sawed in half. This is not true. A sixty-eight team, single-elimination tournament isn't a carefully crafted test of basketball prowess. It is contrived chaos, like sixty-seven spins of a roulette wheel. Upsets abound in the bloated tournament's sixty-seven games, and the tournament becomes a test of lucky survival rather than a test of quality. In this real-life version of the fairy tale, the cruel stepsisters win the prince's affections with alarming regularity.

2. Once upon a time, the ACC was the only conference that staged a post season tournament to determine a champion that was to receive the conference's automatic bid to the NCAA tournament. Now all the conferences are doing it and the post season conference tournaments water down the NCAA tournament field. This season, twelve regular season champions of single bid conferences—teams that had proven themselves best over a grueling home-and-away schedule—were eliminated from the NCAA Tournament by upsets in their lust-for-money conference tournaments. Only one of those teams won a game in the NCAA tournament.

3. The precept that the best teams should be matched against the weakest teams—No. 1 seeds play No. 16 seeds, No. 2 seeds play No. 15 seeds, etc.—is taken for granted and never challenged, but it creates a self-fulfilling prophecy for the top three seeds. Because they play the weakest competition, the top three seeds have filled 102 of the 136 Final Four slots over the past thirty-four years. Small schools are brainwashed into believing that an invitation to the Big Dance to absorb a first-round mugging at the hands of a major conference school is a rewarding conclusion to a successful season. In the thirty-four history of No. 1 versus No. 16 seeding, UMBC is the only team to avoid the gallows in round one.

No. 1 seeds have a better success rate than No. 2 seeds because they play weaker opponents all the way through the tournament. The following chart depicts the success rates of the various seeds as they progress from round to round:

8	50.0	19.1	0.38	61.5	0.235	62.5	0.147	60.0	0.088	33.3
9	50.0	8.8	0.176	50.0	0.088	33.3	0.029	0.0	0.0	
10	38.2	44.2	0.676	34.8	0.235	12.5	0.029	0.0		
11	37.5	43.1	0.647	40.9	0.264	44.4	0.117			
12	34.5	42.6	0.588	5.0	0.029	0.0				
13	20.6	21.4	0.176	0.0						
14	15.4	9.5	0.058	0.0						
15	5.88	12.5	0.029	0.0						
16	0.7	0.0								

ROUND:	ONE	TWO		SWEET SIXTEEN		ELITE EIGHT		FINAL FOUR		CHAMPIONSHIP GAME
SEED	WIN %	WIN %	AVG. # TEAMS	WIN %	AVG. # TEAMS	WIN %	AVG. # TEAMS	WIN %	AVG. # TEAMS	WIN %
1	99.3	85.9	3.15	81.2	2.76	60.6	1.67	57.9	0.97	63.6
2	94.1	66.4	2.49	72.9	1.83	46.7	0.853	44.8	0.394	38.2
3	84.6	60.9	2.06	48.6	1.0	47.1	0.47	62.5	0.294	40.0
4	79.4	59.3	1.88	34.4	0.627	54.6	0.343	25.0	0.086	33.3
5	65.4	51.7	1.35	17.4	0.24	62.5	0.147	60.0	0.088	0.0
6	62.5	49.4	1.24	30.9	0.383	23.1	0.088	66.7	0.059	50.0
7	61.7	32.1	0.787	33.3	0.265	33.3	0.088	33.3	0.029	100

Note that winning percentages for rounds one and two decline smoothly from high seeds to low seeds. This is no accident. The high seeds win most often because they play the weakest competition in the early rounds. *From the Elite Eight through the Championship game, all seeds have a fair shot at winning the tournament, but No. 1 seeds win most often simply because more of them survive the first three rounds against the weakest opponents.*

4. Since the field is enormous, teams are dispersed across four regional brackets. As a result, the best teams rarely meet in the tournament. No. 1 seeds can't meet a No. 2 or No. 3 seed until the Elite Eight and will never face both. No. 1 seeds can't meet another No. 1 seed until the Final Four. Over the last thirty-four years, the Final Four has hosted an average of 1.67 No. 1 seeds, so they rarely play one another. In 2018, Michigan reached the title game without facing a team seeded higher than No. 6. Of the sixty-seven tournament games this year,

only one game featured two No.1 seeds, and only one game matched a No. 1 against a No. 2. As a result, the best teams rarely prove themselves against the best opponents.

5. When the Committee introduced the pod system, it broke the traditional geographical boundaries of the four regional brackets by mixing brackets across eight locations for rounds one and two. This approach has corrupted the tournament by infusing home court advantage for privileged teams. In 2018, North Carolina, Michigan State, Gonzaga, Kansas and Texas Tech played "home" games while Kentucky, Auburn, Clemson and West Virginia played at sites that were more "away" than neutral. As we saw earlier, home teams enjoy a 7 percent performance advantage and, therefore, the tournament is not a fair test for all teams.

6. The Committee's chronically poor seeding of teams is the final nail in the tournament's coffin. As we've seen, a No. 1 seed is accorded a massive advantage and yet the Committee wrongly selected two of this year's four No.

1 seeds. Kansas benefitted both by receiving a No 1 seed instead of a No. 3 seed and by being placed in "home" location pods. In the Elite Eight, Kansas received a gift from the gods when Duke's last second shot went in and somehow popped back out.

A good tournament ultimately has just two components: a methodology to select and seed teams in the field and clarity of purpose. The NCAA Tournament has both components: A fallible selection committee and the compulsion to make money. Miraculously, the tournament's liability—the repetitious emergence of random champions—has become an asset. The tournament is a game of chance in which all fans can participate vicariously. For better or worse, the NCAA Tournament has evolved into a form of entertainment like a three-week vacation to an amusement park. Unfortunately, this means we cannot call the winner the "National Champion." We can only call that team the NCAA Tournament survivor.

Winning the Office Pool

Given the flaws in the tournament format, the following pointers have stood the test of time in picking winners on a fan's bracket:

1. Ignore the experts. They hype teams and matchups to increase viewership.
2. Ignore Vegas odds. The oddsmakers are not picking winners. They are predicting how fans who are influenced by experts, personal biases, and committee seedings will bet. As bets are placed, the line changes to ensure that the house makes money. The odds do not change based upon the oddsmakers' changing opinions as to which team might win the game.
3. Ignore the committee's seeding of teams. Use the accurate rankings at www. nemosnumbers.com to reseed teams according to strength.
4. Choose a champion from among the top three seeds. You can't beat the odds and you can't win your pool unless you pick the champion.

5. Choose a champion that will play its games at "home."

6. Choose a champion whose path can be cleared by upsets of its toughest potential opponents. Michigan's path to the Final Four was cleared by Florida State which knocked off Xavier and Gonzaga before the Wolverines had to face them.

7. Choose a champion that has a good draw of potential opponents. Opponents that have been overrated comprise a good draw. Opponents whose weaknesses align with the chosen team's strengths comprise a good draw. This year Villanova had the best— easiest—draw and won it all.

8. Fill your bracket so that two No. 1 seeds reach the Final Four and one of them wins the tournament. No. 1 seeds have won more tournaments than all other seeds combined. This year Kansas and Villanova reached the Final Four.

9. Fill the Sweet Sixteen round of your bracket with three No. 1 seeds, two and a half No. 2 seeds, two No. 3 seeds, and two No.

4 seeds. Complete that round with the bracket-busting lower seeds of your choice, and/or add another No. 2 seed. Resist the temptation to advance those infamous No. 12 seeds to the later rounds. After pulling the shocking upset in round one, they win less than half the time in round two and have won only once in the Sweet Sixteen. Stick to seeds five through eight. After that, make your picks according to the rankings at www.nemosnumbers.com.

10. Remember that the NCAA Tournament crowns a survivor and not a winner. A deep bench becomes an asset from the second weekend through the championship game. Over and over, good teams with a short bench run out of gas during the second weekend.

Good luck!

Chapter Nine
Cinderella's Ball

Turn and peep, turn and peep,
There's blood within the shoe,
The shoe it is too small for her,
The true bride waits for you.
—**FROM** *CINDERELLA* **BY JACOB AND**
WILHELM GRIMM

If the NCAA wanted to construct a tournament that would more often identify Cinderella and prevent her evil sisters from winning the prince's heart, it would follow the example of the College World Series. College baseball does just about everything correctly. Unlike NCAA basketball, which compels high school graduates to spend a year in college before turning professional, college baseball gives graduating high schoolers a choice between a professional career and a college education. That is the same right that all graduating nonathletes have. If a graduate accepts a college baseball scholarship, he is bound to college life for three years, which is the same as the commitment a scholarship football player makes. I've never heard a convincing reason for the arcane basketball rule but suspect money is the demon.

As a prelude to the College World Series, the NCAA stages Regional and Super Regional tournaments, akin to basketball pods, and the eight winners assemble in a truly neutral location, Omaha, Nebraska, to play a double elimination championship round. If the NCAA was interested in correcting the flaws in the Big Dance, it would adopt a similar pattern.

A field of thirty-two teams—the best thirty-two teams in the country without regard for conference affiliation or conference titles—could play in eight pods scattered around the country. The pod format could copy the soccer format for groups and play round-robin. The eight pod winners would then assemble at a neutral site—perhaps rotating locations as for the Super Bowl—and play a double elimination championship series.

This format would ensure that teams pulling fluke early-round upsets are not rewarded with advancement to the Elite Eight unless they can upset higher-seeded teams more than once. This format would ensure that great teams are not eliminated by a single fluke upset. This format would ensure that the best teams would play other good teams more than once.

The proliferation of conference tournaments that award the automatic NCAA berth to the conference tournament winner, eliminate deserving regular season champions and replace them with lucky tournament winners. Conference tournaments marginalize regular season results and dilute the NCAA tournament product. To become a truly fair test of championship greatness, the automatic berths in the NCAA tournament must go to regular season conference champions. Those teams have proven themselves over a sixteen-to-eighteen game home-and-away schedule.

The NCAA and the television networks would lose no revenue with this plan. The same number of games could be televised, and the games would arguably be more competitive and more meaningful. When the NCAA Tournament field was expanded to sixty-four teams, the NCAA gave away the most compelling attribute of any product for sale—exclusivity. If anyone can have it, it's not valuable. This format would restore a measure of exclusivity.

What of the thirty-six teams that would no longer go to the Big Dance? They could be invited to a real National Invitation Tournament (NIT) tournament where they could win a game or two as a reward for an excellent season.

The prescription for a better tournament is obvious, but change won't happen unless you, the fan, apply pressure on the NCAA to make the obvious changes.

~The End~

About the Author

Mike Nemeth is a retired Information Technology executive living in the Atlanta suburbs with his wife, Angie, and their rescue dog, Sophie. His previous works include the Amazon Bestselling crime thriller, *Defiled*.

Morgan James
Speakers Group

We connect Morgan James published
authors with live and online events
and audiences who will benefit
from their expertise.

Morgan James makes all of our titles
available through the Library for All
Charity Organization.

www.LibraryForAll.org

Printed in the USA
CPSIA information can be obtained
at www.ICGtesting.com
JSHW080002150824
68134JS00021B/2236